Mother Nature's Children

by Genevieve Vaughan
Illustrated by Liliana Wilson

Mother Nature's Children

Anomaly Press
P. O. Box 3138
Austin, TX 78764
www.gift-economy.com

ISBN 0-9672912-2-4 English
ISBN 0-9672912-3-2 Spanish

Printed in the United States of America
at Morgan Printing in Austin, Texas

This book is dedicated to Margie First
with thanks for her many years of loving care
for Stonehaven and all its visitors,
both human and animal.

This book was written in an attempt to show how two world views, one based on gift giving and the other on exchange, interact and conflict with each other in our daily lives. The two world views are caught up with the definition of gender, especially the socialization of boys towards the values of dominance and competition. Capitalism also functions on these "masculinist" values and for that reason we can say that capitalism is patriarchal.

Gift giving is a logic practiced by everyone in many areas of life, but it is particularly visible in the unilateral caregiving of mothers toward their children, without which the children would not survive. Exchange is a logic in which one person satisfies the needs of another only so that s/he will get her own needs satisfied. Gift giving is directed towards the needs of the other person, and gives value to the receiver. Exchange requires calculation and measurement of the goods given and received. It places people in an adversarial situation in which each tries to get more than the other. It is ego-oriented rather than other-oriented.

Scarcity is created by allowing a few to accumulate a lot while most people live in poverty. In fact, if everyone were living in abundance they would not need to exchange but could satisfy each others' needs by gift giving. Scarcity makes gift giving difficult. Nature is the great gift giver, but it is being privatized and commodified at every turn, polluted and cemented over, so that many people live in a non-natural, non-gift giving environment where the needs of the market are more important than the needs of people. We are not usually conscious of how much the exchange logic hurts us and that the solution to our problems is to return to ways of interacting based on direct gift giving.

The Country

"Oh! Hello, Aunt Lilly! We're so glad we've come to see you!" said the boys as they jumped out of the car.

"Well, I'm glad to see you, too! We have some wonderful days ahead of us for your vacation," Aunt Lilly said as she gave the boys each a big hug.

Brandon and Kolton's dad got their suitcases out of the trunk of the car and brought them into the house.

"Okay, then," said the boys' father as he gave them and Lilly each a kiss.

"Bye, Dad!" said Brandon!

"Bye, Daddy!" said Kolton. (He always called his father Daddy because he was littlest.)

"We'll see you in four days," said Lilly.

"We have an in-town day and an out-of-town day," she went on. "We're going to Stonehaven Ranch tomorrow. The next day we'll stay in town and do whatever you like."

The next day the boys got up early, as soon as they heard the birds chirping outside Aunt Lilly's window. The sun was shining. It was going to be a beautiful day.

Lilly fixed the boys some wonderful pancakes for breakfast. Brandon liked honey on his pancakes. Kolton liked molasses.

They all got in Aunt Lilly's car. "Are there going to be horses on Stonehaven Ranch?" they asked.

STONEHAVEN

“Yes, little bitty horses,” Aunt Lilly answered. “And something else. A great big funny looking bird.”

“Big Bird,” said Kolton, who had been watching Sesame Street.

“No,” said Lilly. “Not a TV character, a real bird. It’s called an emu.”

“I want to play with the emu,” said Brandon.

“Me, too! Me, too!” said Kolton.

Soon they were driving through the gate at Stonehaven. “There’s the sign,” said Lilly.

As they drove up to the house, they saw Margie standing on the steps waving at them. “Welcome, boys,” she said. “Its nice for city boys to come here where they get to be with Mother Nature.”

“Who’s that?” said Kolton.

“Oh, Mother Nature,” said Margie, “she’s a spirit, the spirit of giving. She touches everyone who comes here with her magic. If you open up your mind’s eyes maybe you’ll get to see her.”

“I want to see the horses first,” said Brandon.

“I want to go see Big Bird first,” said Kolton.

“How about going swimming first?” said Margie.

“Swimming! Yes! Yes!” yelled both the boys enthusiastically. They got into their suits and jumped into the pool.

“Hey, look!” cried Brandon, “Emus!” The huge birds were standing looking at them from behind the fence.

“And little bitty horses. Over there!” yelled Kolton. The little horses had poked their noses through another fence to sniff at them.

Kolton blew bubbles in the water. Brandon made big splashes. Aunt Lilly, who was an artist, relaxed in the sunshine and drew pictures.

Margie came over to the pool with her hands full of apples and carrots. “Who wants to feed the emus?” she asked. “I do! I do!” both boys replied.

As Margie and the boys came up to the fence, the emus pranced around with their great big feet.

“They’re doing a dance!” said Kolton.

Brandon held out a carrot, and one of the emus stuck its neck way out and grabbed the carrot in its beak. It gulped that carrot right down. Kolton hid behind Margie. The other emus all came and stuck their necks out, too. Margie gave Kolton a piece of celery. The emu grabbed one end, and Kolton held on to the other.

“Let it go, let it go!” cried Margie. Kolton did, and the emu happily ate the celery. Brandon gave each emu a piece of apple.

“Look how much they like apples,” he grinned.

Lilly drew a picture of Brandon, Kolton, and an emu. Here it is. Can you tell which is which?

"The little horses like apples, too," said Margie. "Put on your shoes and we'll go feed them."

The boys got their shoes on. They had to walk over some stickery ground to get to the fence. The boys wanted to pat the miniature horses' soft noses, but the horses wanted the apples right away. Margie showed the boys how to hold their hands flat with the apples on them so the horses couldn't bite them by mistake.

"This horse is named Goldy," said Margie, "and this one is Silver Bell."

Lilly drew a picture of the boys and the horses. Can you tell which is which?

"I bet you're hungry, too," said Margie. "I have some lunch ready. Let's go in and eat."

"Put your clothes on before lunch," Aunt Lilly said. "When we finish eating we're going to explore the cave."

"I really want to explore the cave," said Brandon. "Is it dark?"

"Is it scary?" asked Kolton.

"Yes, it's dark," said Margie, "but it's not scary. I'll give you some flashlights. I've been in there lots of times."

The boys got dressed and came inside. They all sat down at the table and ate the delicious vegetable soup and grilled cheese sandwiches Margie had made for them.

"Well," Margie asked, "did anybody see Mother Nature when we were outside?"

"I saw her when you were feeding the emus," said Lilly, "and I drew a picture of her. Here it is."

"Hey, I saw her when we were feeding the horses!" Brandon chimed in.

"She's always there when we're feeding animals—or people," said Margie.

“Hey, there she is right now!” cried Kolton. “She’s standing right behind Margie. I can see her with my mind’s eyes.”

“All the vegetables in this soup are gifts of Mother Nature,” said Margie. “I picked them in the garden. They’re all free.”

“You didn’t have to pay for them?” asked Brandon.

“Not a penny,” said Margie.

“I like free vegetables!” said Kolton.

"Thank you, Mother Nature," said Brandon.

"Hey! Listen to that," said Lilly. "I can hear her saying, You're welcome!"

A bird outside was singing a beautiful song.

"That's the way she talks sometimes," said Lilly.

Margie gave Lilly and Brandon and Kolton each a flashlight. "It's dark inside the cave," she said.

"Do we have to buy tickets?" asked Brandon.

"Do we have to wait in line? asked Kolton.

"No you don't have to buy anything. You don't have to wait in line, and you can stay as long as you want," laughed Margie.

"This is not an amusement park," said Lilly.

"No," said Margie, "it's a real cave, and it's always open. It's been there a million years. You'll find it back behind my house by the big tree." Margie gave Lilly a piece of paper with some words written on it. "Here, this is the song we wrote for the cave xylophone. Take it with you. You'll see what I mean."

Lilly and the two boys picked up their flashlights and walked across the field, past Margie's house.

"There's the big tree!" yelled Brandon as he started to run. Kolton ran, too.

The opening to the cave was small and dark. Lilly had to crouch down to get through, but the boys wiggled through easily. It was cool inside the cave and smelled musty.

They all turned their flashlights on.

"I'm kind of scared," said Lilly.

"I'll help you, Aunt Lilly," said Brandon as he took her hand.

"Me too," said Kolton as he held onto her shirt.

They shined their lights on a sort of doorway. "I think there are bats in there," said Lilly. "Margie told me. Let's go the other way."

They walked down a passageway until they came to a chamber that had stalactites hanging from the ceiling and stalagmites coming up from the floor. There was another room next to it with stalactites on the wall. There was a hole in the wall. Kolton shined his flashlight in the hole.

"We could go in there," said Brandon. "We're small enough."

"Oh! No you couldn't," cried Lilly. "I wouldn't be able to get you out."

"Let's not," said Kolton.

"Okay, lets not," said Brandon.

Somebody had left a candle in the middle of the floor with some matches nearby. Lilly said, "Lets light the candle and turn off our flashlights. Then we'll see how it used to be for people who lived in caves a long time ago in prehistory."

She lit the candle, and they turned off the flashlights. They sat on the floor. It was very, very quiet. The candlelight cast shadows on the wall.

"I like this," said Kolton. Lilly said, "Let's blow out the candle and see what it's like in the dark. Keep your flashlights ready so you can turn them back on again when you want to." It was really dark in the cave without even the candlelight.

"Wow!" said Brandon.

"Wow!" said Kolton.

"Are you scared?" asked Lilly.

"No, it's awesome," said Brandon.

"I think it's awesome, too," said Kolton.

"It's like being inside of Mother Nature," said Lilly.

They turned their flashlights back on again. Lilly started looking at the stalactites on the wall. There was a stick nearby.

Lilly said, “I wonder if this is what Margie meant by the cave xylophone.” She picked up the stick and tapped the stalactites lightly. They made sounds.

“You can play music on these!” she exclaimed.

“Let me try,” said Brandon.

“Be careful,” said Lilly. “You don’t want to damage anything.”

Brandon tapped the stalactites and played a little tune.

“You try too,” he said to Kolton as he handed him the stick. Kolton played a little tune.

“Margie and her friends made up the song that’s on this piece of paper she gave me,” said Lilly.

“Its the song of the cave.” She took the stick, and then read the words and tapped on the stalactites as she sang...

I've been here
A million years
And I'm living still.
Come to me
I'll set you free
And all your wishes fill.

The tune was sort of like "Love Me Tender." Lilly sang the song a couple of times, and then the boys sang it with her.

"That's what the cave says," Lilly explained. "You'll be able to remember it later."

"Let's go back now," said Lilly. "Margie said we could groom the horses."

Brandon and Kolton sang the cave song all the way back to the house.

Margie showed Lilly and the boys where the horses' brushes and combs were kept. She said, "The horses love to be groomed. They get lots of sticker burrs in their manes and tails. And they love to be brushed."

First both boys worked on Silver Bell. Then they worked on Goldy.

"Those horses are shining like silver and gold," said Lilly.

"Horses are even better than silver and gold," said Brandon.

"Yes, because they're alive" said Kolton.

"That's why we have to take good care of them," said Lilly.

"I like taking care of things," said Kolton.

"I like helping Margie," said Brandon.

"Those horses look beautiful," said Margie as she came up to where they were standing. She had brought some more apples for the boys to feed to the horses. "Thank you so much for helping me take care of them."

"It's time for us to go now," said Lilly. "Give the horses a hug."

"Bye, Silver Bell! Bye, Goldy!" the boys said as they hugged the horses' necks.

Then Margie said, “Hey, give me a hug, too.” The boys hugged her, and so did Lilly.

“Thank you so much for such a wonderful day,” said Lilly.

“Thank you, Margie,” said Brandon.

“Thank you, Margie and Mother Nature,” said Kolton.

“You’re welcome,” Margie said. “Come back soon.”

The City

The next day the boys got up late. The sun was already streaming in the windows.

"Lets go back to the country again today," said Kolton as the boys were eating their breakfast.

"No," Lilly said. "Today we're going to stay in town, but you can choose what you want to do unless it's something I really don't like doing."

"Let's go to the Mall! Let's go to the Mall!" both boys shouted.

"Oh, I'm sorry," said Lilly "That's one thing I really don't like to do. Choose something else."

"The movies! The movies!" the boys said.

"Okay," said Lilly. "Anything else?"

"Let's go play miniature golf," said Brandon.

"Let's go to the park," said Kolton.

"Okay, okay, okay," Lilly said. "Let's plan it out. The movies start in the afternoon, and we can go to the park any time. So let's start with miniature golf this morning."

"It costs a lot of money," said Brandon as they got ready to leave.

"Don't forget your purse," said Kolton.

JOLLY
LEPRECHAUN
MINI
GOLF COURSE
WIN
$10 ADULTS $8 CHILDREN
COURSE
2
DO NOT ENTER
COURSE
1

It was a beautiful day. The sun was shining as they drove up to the Jolly Leprechaun Miniature Golf Course. The ticket office and restrooms were located in the green painted trousers of a giant leprechaun with a fat stomach, a white beard, and a bright red shirt. The leprechaun was holding a giant golden golf club.

"That's ten dollars for you and eight dollars for each of the boys for the first thirty minutes, Ma'am," said the man at the ticket office. "Then you get to the Pot of Gold." He gave them each a score card, a golf club, and a ball. Lilly paid, and they walked through the gate.

"Now, the point is to get your ball into the hole in the least number of hits," said Lilly.

"The point is to win the game," said Brandon.

"I want to win, too!" said Kolton.

The first hole was a slope with a sort of spiral at the bottom. Brandon started. He got his ball in the hole in five strokes. Kolton got his ball in the hole in three, and Lilly in three.

"You guys were lucky," said Brandon.

The next part of the course had a pond in the middle of it. When Brandon hit his ball, it ended up right in the middle of the pond. The sign on the side of the pond said, penalty three strokes. Kolton hit his ball hard and it jumped right over the pond, but Lilly's ball went into the water behind Brandon's. Both of them had to fish their balls out and lose three strokes.

The rest of that part was so easy Kolton only took one more stroke to put his ball in the hole. Brandon and Lilly each took two. They wrote their scores down on their score cards.

"I've already got 11," said Brandon.

"I have 9," said Lilly, "and Kolton, you only have 5. You're winning so far."

"We better hurry up," Brandon said. "We only have 30 minutes and we've still got three more holes."

In the next part of the course there were four mechanical leprechaun statues bending back and forth. They were painted like the jolly leprechaun at the entrance but were much smaller. You could hear the clicks and hums of their machinery. Brandon and Kolton both got started pretty well, but when Lilly took aim this time she got her ball in the hole in only one stroke.

"Oh no!" said Brandon, "I'm getting beaten by a girl!"

"Sissy, sissy, sissy!" sang Kolton.

"Well, you're a sissy too, then!" yelled Brandon.

"Lets count our points again," said Kolton.

Lilly counted. "Let's see, Brandon has 15, I have 10, and Kolton only has 8. Kolton's winning."

"I'm winning! I'm winning!" Kolton chanted. "I'm winning, and you're a sissy," he taunted Brandon.

Brandon just scowled and started hitting the ground in front of him with the golf club.

"Let's go on," said Lilly. "I want to get to the Pot of Gold."

There was a sand pit in the middle of the next part of the course. Brandon's ball went into the sand and so did Lilly's. Only Kolton's went all the way to the other side. Every time Brandon tried to hit the ball, the sand flew up everywhere and the ball just barely jumped. He took four more strokes to get the ball in the hole. Lilly took three, and Kolton only took two more.

"Hey, I'm winning again!" Kolton yelled.

"I hate you!" Brandon screamed at Kolton. "I wish you'd never been born."

"Come on, Brandon. What a mean thing to say to your brother. Be a good sport," said Lilly. "Calm down. We're almost at the Pot of Gold. We have to hurry, too. Our time is almost up."

The last part of the course had a big gold ring the players had to hit their balls through. Behind it was a big arrow with a sign saying this way to the pot of gold. Brandon got his ball through the ring in three strokes, Lilly in three, and Kolton this time in four. On their score cards they wrote the grand totals: Brandon had 22 points, Lilly 17, and Kolton 14.

"Well, Kolton won. Congratulations, Kolton," said Lilly.

"Yeah. Big deal," said Brandon.

"Don't feel so bad, Brandon. Maybe you'll win the next one," said Kolton.

They followed the arrow toward the Pot Of Gold. It was a huge pot, almost as big as the giant Jolly Leprechaun at the entrance. There was another ticket office in the front of the pot. They could hear music and mechanical laughter coming from behind a brightly painted fence.

"You ain't seen nothing yet," said the ticket man. "This part of the course is even better than the first part. You can take a whole hour, and there are prizes for the winners at the end."

"Can we do it, Aunt Lilly? Please, please," begged Kolton.

"How much is it?" asked Lilly.

"Just like the first part," said the man. "Ten dollars for you, and eight dollars for each of the boys."

"Kolton, I think we should leave. It's too much," said Aunt Lilly.

“Oh, but I might win. I want to get the prize,” Kolton was almost starting to cry.

“It costs too much,” said Lilly. “Besides, I think you two are tired.

“I’m not tired,” said Kolton.

“Who cares about this dumb miniature golf course?” said Brandon. “Only sissies and babies win at it anyway.”

“Make up your mind, Lady,” said the ticket man. “Buy your tickets or leave. The exit is that way.”

“Lets go, boys,” said Lilly as she took Kolton’s hand. Kolton was crying as they got back into the car.

“I wanted to win the pot of gold,” he said. “And I’m not a sissy OR a baby.”

“Then stop crying like one,” said Brandon.

Kolton stopped crying.

$10 ADULTS $8 CHILDREN
MINI GOLF
CLUBS BALLS
WIN
WIN

"Where shall we go for lunch?" asked Lilly brightly.

"Let's go to Big One's," Brandon suggested.

"Yes. I want to go to Big One's," Kolton agreed.

Big One's is the one
That makes you have fun

they began to sing together.

"That's the advertising song, Aunt Lilly," explained Brandon. "We learned it from TV."

"Yes, I've heard it," Lilly replied. "I think there's a Big One's down this street somewhere," she said as she drove. "Tell me if you see the golden 1."

"There it is down there, Aunt Lilly," Brandon pointed out.

"That golden 1 looks like the gold golf club at the Jolly Leprechaun," said Kolton.

"And the restaurant looks like the pot of gold," said Brandon. The restaurant actually was painted gold.

"What do you want to eat?" asked Lilly as they stood in line to place their order.

“I want lots of golden 1s,” said Kolton.

“They’re these special French fried potatoes,” Brandon explained.

“I want a double Booper with cheese and a soda,” he told the overworked young woman at the counter when it was their turn to order.”

“I want a cheese chili gooey Booper,” said Kolton, “and lots of golden 1s”.

“I’m a vegetarian. I’ll just have a salad and some water,” said Lilly as she paid the check.

“Coming right up,” said the young woman. “And for you boys, here are some free He Man cutouts you can play with while you wait.”

They found a table and sat down.

“Hey look. My He Man has a bazooka,” said Brandon.

“Mine has a machine gun. He’s Mr. Big One,” said Kolton.

“A bazooka is stronger than a machine gun,” said Brandon.

“No, a machine gun is stronger.”

“Let’s play war and see who gets to be Mr. Big One,” suggested Brandon.

“Please play quietly,” said Lilly. “And please don’t play war. I hate war.”

“That’s just because you’re a girl,” said Brandon. He pointed his gun at the waiter who was bringing their tray.

“Big One’s loves us because they give us these free He Man toys,” said Kolton. “This is the best restaurant in the whole wide world!”

“They’re not giving it to us free. They’re just trying to get us to come here so they can make money on us,” said Lilly”

“Well, they got me,” said Kolton.

“I like the food,” said Brandon. “Well, and the toys. Why are you a vegetarian, Aunt Lilly?”

“I just don’t like to kill animals” said Lilly.

“We have to eat red meat to grow up to be he men,” said Kolton.

“Being a vegetarian is all right for girls,” said Brandon.

HAVE
GOLDEN
FRIES
HAVE
A
BOOPER
BURGER
JUMBO
DRINKS

When the boys finished their lunch, they were ready to go to the movies. They decided to go to a film that was showing at a theater not far away, called *Money, Men and Monsters*.

“I want lots of money when I grow up so I can be a monster,” said Kolton as they stood in line to buy their tickets.

“I want lots of money so I can go to the front of the line,” said Brandon.

“We didn’t have to stand in line at the cave,” remembered Kolton.”

“Even if you have money you can’t be a monster,” said Aunt Lilly. “I won’t let you. And you can’t go to the front of the line. I won’t let you do that, either.”

Lilly paid for their tickets and then bought the boys some popcorn and sodas. As they sat down in the darkened theater, the advertising was just beginning for a show about war.

"Hey, cool!" said Brandon as bombs exploded and bodies flew in all directions.

"Yuck!" said Kolton.

"Hey, Kolton, be a He Man," said Brandon.

"Boom, bang, bang, bang!" yelled Kolton.

An ad came on for popcorn. Brandon and Kolton pelted each other with pieces of popcorn.

"Bang! Bang! Bang! Boom!" they yelled. "It's a popcorn war!"

"Shhh," said Lilly.

People in front of them were beginning to turn around.

"Stop that, or I'm taking you home," Lilly scolded.

The main feature was starting. The boys calmed down. The movie was a story about two men—brothers—who raised monsters to use in horror shows.

“Hey, they’re brothers just like us,” said Kolton.

The plot thickened as the monsters got loose and began to devastate the city. The men told the mayor that if the city gave them each a million dollars they would call off the monsters.

“Hey cool. They’re going to make a lot of money,” said Brandon.

The brothers in the movie threw electric shocks at the monsters.

“I can do that,” yelled Kolton.

“Yeah, right!” jeered Brandon, as the monsters began to chase the men. “Lets pretend all these pieces of popcorn are little people. Then we’ll eat them.

“That’s terrible,” said Lilly. “How would you like it if somebody ate you?”

“I don’t want anybody to eat me,” said Kolton.

“Shhh back there,” said a man in front of them.

When the movie was over Lilly waited for the boys outside the restroom. There was a video game machine on the wall with monsters on it.

“Hey, Aunt Lilly,” said Brandon as he and Kolton came through the door, “I want to play that video game.”

“No,” Aunt Lilly said. “I can’t stand this war and monster stuff anymore,”

“I’m a monster, and I’m going to destroy you if you won’t let me play the video game,” Brandon growled.

“Come on, let’s get out of here,” Lilly said firmly as she took both boys by the hands and led them out of the movie theater into the afternoon sunlight.

"Now we're going to the park," Lilly said as they got in the car.

They drove to a beautiful green field that sloped down to a river. There was a huge outcropping of rock in the middle of the field that children liked to play on.

"I'll race you to the rocks," said Lilly. She ran the fastest, after all.

"I knew you'd beat us because you're grown up," puffed Kolton as he got to the rocks.

"I'll just sit here in the shade of the tree while you climb," said Lilly.

"I want to sit down a minute, too," said Brandon.

"I want to lie down on the grass," said Kolton as he climbed down the rocks.

All three of them stretched out on the grass and looked up at the sky through the leaves of the tree. A breeze was blowing, and a bird was singing in the tree.

"Hey! Listen to that bird," said Brandon.

"Do you think Mother Nature is here?" asked Kolton.

"Yes, she's here," said Lilly. "See, she's painting pictures in the sky. Look at the clouds."

"That cloud looks like a bird," said Kolton.

"It looks like a monster to me," said Brandon.

"Mother Nature wouldn't paint monsters," said Lilly.

"Okay," said Brandon. "I see a flying horse over there."

"It looks like a flying horse to me, too," said Lilly.

"Me, too," said Kolton.

The boys got up and went to climb on the rocks. There were lots of holes and secret passageways. Kolton was smaller, so he could get through more easily.

“Come on, Brandon. I’ll help you,” he said as he held out his hand.

“Thanks, little brother,” said Brandon “You’re a good kid after all.”

Both boys got to the top of the rocks and waved to Aunt Lilly, who had gotten out her sketch book and was drawing again.

“It’s like when we were at Stonehaven,” said Brandon.

“There are no monsters here,” said Kolton.

That night as Lilly was putting the boys to bed Kolton said, “The park was just like Stonehaven.”

“Yes, everything was free there,” said Brandon.

“I saw Mother Nature smiling,” said Kolton.

“Go to sleep now and dream about Mother Nature,” said Lilly. Tomorrow you can tell your mom and dad about everything we’ve done.”

“Good night, Aunt Lilly,” said the boys.

“Sweet dreams,” said Lilly. “Everything you dream about is free, too,” she reminded them as she blew them a kiss and turned out the light.